DEALING WITH DISAPPOINTMENT

Restore Your Hope, Faith, & Passion

ISBN 978-1-621660-89-7

Published by XP Publishing, a department of XP Ministries
PO Box 1017, Maricopa, AZ 85139. XPpublishing.com

DEALING WITH DISAPPOINTMENT

Restore Your Hope, Faith, & Passion

Bart Hadaway

ACKNOWLEDGEMENTS

Thank you to God first and foremost for the opportunity to share in this book. In the midst of failures, shortcomings, struggles, and even battles with hopelessness and cynicisms, He has always been there to encourage me. His Word brought to me by the Holy Spirit has been constant. Thank You, Father.

Next I would like to thank my wife of thirty-two years. We have been blessed with a marriage truly made in heaven though we have had our share of trials. Kim, through it all there has never been a time when you were not faithful, loving, and encouraging to me. I love you.

I want to thank my children. There is no way we could have been more blessed. Andrea, Ashlee, and Jared, I love you with all my heart. The only hint you could have of my love for you would be through your love for your own children (Which, by the way, I am so grateful for. Keep them coming!).

To all those in my life who have inspired me, thank you. Over the years, one of my greatest joys is the amazing people God has brought into my life. Through the constant love and support of my parents and siblings and the body of Christ, I have been truly blessed. Though the body of Christ is far from perfect, how thankful I am for all the love and goodness she has given to me.

To every pastor and leader who have taken the time to pour into my life, you mean more to me than you will ever know.

I especially want to thank Patricia, Ron, and the XP team. You are amazing. The years of serving with you have been some of the best of my life.

Rob, you are a once in a lifetime friend.

There are many others that I could name individually, but I will stop here due to book space. I love you all!

It is my prayer that this book will bring healing and hope to your heart, renew your passion and focus, and regain your fight.

CONTENTS

FOREWORD

Patricia King

Life is full of disappointments and everyone experiences them. Therefore, it is important to deal effectively with them – to make them work for you and not against you!

I admire Walt Disney, creator of Mickey Mouse. When he first began to develop "Mickey," he suffered three failures and the last was a complete bankruptcy. One failure alone would have been disappointing but three would be devastating for most of us. After each disappointing failure, he continued to work on the development of his animated mouse. The fourth attempt brought his breakthrough.

Mickey Mouse is now probably the most famous animated character in the world, and even though Walt

Disney has passed on, Mickey lives. After the creation of Mickey, Walt gave birth to many other characters along with Disneyland, Disneyworld, as well as countless movies and enterprises. Mr. Walt Disney overcame disappointments. He refused to allow them to hold him back.

King David in the Bible also overcame disappointment. When he returned to Ziklag, everything was destroyed, lost, and captured. He was overwhelmed with disappointment and devastation in the midst of it all, but he knew how to go to the Lord with his pain. As he poured his heart out before the Lord, he received direction to overcome the tragic situation: The Lord said, "Pursue, overtake, and recover all" (1 Samuel 30:8). David rose up in the midst of his despair and did exactly what the Lord told him to do. As a result, his victory became one of the most outstanding testimonies in the Word.

Like you, I have had my share of disappointments throughout life. Disappointments are never pleasant and sometimes are extremely painful, but in the midst of each disappointment, there is an invitation from the Lord to intentionally rise up and move on. I have learned so much from the Lord in times of disappointment as He has taken me deep into His heart, revealed profound truths, and offered nuggets of wisdom. He truly does give you the "treasures of darkness and the secret wealth of hidden places" (Isaiah 45:3).

Bart Hadaway is a champion in the Lord and has helped many walk through their times of disappointments and trials. His book will give you encouraging scriptural insights to help you overcome disappointments and move on with fresh hope and faith.

My prayer for you, my friend, is that you come to know His comfort, healing, strength, and love in your times of disappointment. His invitation is for you to journey from strength to strength and from glory to glory—and you will. Nothing can hold you back! Nothing!

"Forgetting what lies behind and reaching forward to what lies ahead, I press on toward the goal for the prize of the upward call of God in Christ Jesus" (Philippians 3:13-14).

You are loved!

PATRICIA KING
FOUNDER OF XPMINISTRIES

INTRODUCTION

God first appeared to Abram in Mesopotamia and made him a promise: "I will make a great nation of you through your descendants." Now, this was quite a promise because Abram's wife Sarai was barren – they had no children and had given up hope on the possibility. Abram believed God and obeyed Him, but then many, many years passed... and still no children.

Abram and his wife were old, way past the point that Sarai should be able to conceive a child, when God appeared to Abram again to confirm His promise to give Abram many descendants. By then, Abram had lost hope that he would have a son of his own, so he had some serious questions for God. However, when God reassured Abram of His promise,

Abram made the choice to believe in God's goodness and His words (Genesis 15:6). He began to hope again.

Yet it was at least another fourteen years before Isaac finally was born! Abraham waited over twenty-five years for God's promise to come to pass. In the natural, it seemed impossible. But with God, all things are possible!

Primarily, this book is about hope — a hope founded in the bedrock of the goodness of God. An unshakeable confidence in His goodness will keep us filled with hope even when the storms and disappointments of life assault and at times, overwhelm us. Emotions will rise and fall but our hope can remain intact.

It is the supernatural faith of God that produces steadfast hope, and it is this hope that described Abraham when it was said of him, "Even when there was no reason for hope, Abraham kept hoping" (Romans 4:18 NLT).

Hope in this biblical context is much more than merely desiring for something to happen. In Greek, the word hope is *elpis*, and it infers pleasurable anticipation; it is the expectation or confidence that something actually is going to happen. That is the hope that sustains us!

THE GOODNESS OF GOD

The glory of God **IS** His *goodness;* it is the fullness of all He is. God promises that His glory and the knowledge of

> An unshakeable confidence in His goodness will keep us filled
> with hope even when the storms and disappointments of life
> assault and at times, overwhelm us. Emotions will rise and
> fall but our hope can remain intact.

His glory will cover the earth (Numbers 14:21, Habakkuk
2:14), but He intends for that glory and goodness to be received and experienced by us first – His sons and daughters.
Then, out of this experience, we partner with God to reveal
His goodness in all the earth. As believers, when we lose our
hope, the glory and goodness of God are stifled within, and
others are kept from seeing it manifest. No wonder the enemy assaults the goodness of God with such fierceness!

The characteristics of God that spring out of His goodness are infinite. Within His goodness are His love, faithfulness, and mercy – everything wonderful about who He is.
When you are established in the truth of His goodness, you
will remain strong in hope no matter what comes your way.

Psalm 42 is a powerful chapter that reveals a man desperate for God. King David experienced the heights of God's
presence, power, and goodness, but now he finds himself in
the pit of despair. However, in the midst of that despair, he
chooses to remember and focus on the goodness of God. He

made the *choice* to believe. He made the *choice* to praise. He made the *choice* to hope. Twice in this chapter he actually commanded himself to hope in God (42:5, 11).

It is never wrong to pour out your heart to God (Psalm 62:8), and it is not wrong to ask Him for help or to bring change to a situation. But ultimately, our hope must simply be based upon who He is, regardless of circumstances.

As you read this book, be as King David: encourage and strengthen yourself in the Lord (1 Samuel 30:6). Command yourself to hope in God, and declare in your heart, "I will hope continually" (Psalm 71:14).

In *The Shawshank Redemption*, there's a scene that takes place in a prison yard. Two convicts are leaning against a wall while they talk. One is serving a life sentence for a murder he committed, and the other is serving a life sentence for a murder he did not commit. Andy, the man who was unjustly convicted says, "Hope is a good thing — maybe the best of things — so get busy living, or get busy dying."

What do you say? Come on. Let's get busy living!

1

BREAK THE STRONGHOLD OF UNBELIEF

FROM TIME TO TIME, we all face the painful experience of disappointment. Jesus said that in this world we would have tribulation, but He also encouraged us to be hopeful because He has overcome the world.

A few years back, I heard the Lord say, "The stronghold of unbelief is sown in the seed of disappointment." God showed me that every time we experience disappointment, the enemy is there to sow his seeds of doubt, accusation, and unbelief, which ultimately develop into hopelessness.

As a young believer many years ago, I went through an experience that affected me for a long time. While knocking on doors one Saturday, my wife and I led a young couple to the Lord. As our friendship developed, we discovered that the husband was in a battle for his life – he was fighting cancer. He invited me to go with him to a prayer meeting where they were going to pray for his healing. I had never been around anything like this, but I wanted to go and support him. While I was unfamiliar with supernatural healing at this stage of my walk with God, I definitely wanted my friend to be healed. At the meeting, the leader instructed any who had any unbelief to not join in prayer. He said, "We don't want you to hinder our prayers." A bit fearful, I backed up – I certainly did not want to be a hindrance to my friend's healing! Despite all the prayer, a short time later, my friend died.

The resulting disappointment and confusion continued to impact me for years. At first I did not realize just how much, but as I grew in my walk with the Lord, I began to notice that anytime I prayed for someone's healing, there was a stinging reality of unbelief in me. Praise God, He showed me that unbelief entered my life during this experience with my friend, and He broke the stronghold off of my life.

Disappointment comes in many forms and many ways. When we don't properly respond to disappointment, the result is always the same: a sick heart. We see this pattern in Proverbs:

- By sorrow of the heart the spirit is broken (15:13).

- A broken spirit dries the bones (17:22).

- Who can bear a broken spirit (18:14)?

- Hope deferred (disappointment) makes the heart sick (13:12).

Unmet expectations can cause pain, and an unhealed heart always leads to hopelessness. Disappointments and sick hearts have drastically reduced the expectations of many of God's people and as a result, they live far below the abundant life God has provided.

Graham Cooke has said that most of God's people live simply trying to get their needs met instead of living in the inheritance which God has already provided. In order to really live, we need to allow our pain and disappointments to find healing in the truth from God's perspective. We must render disappointment powerless.

When we suffer with wounds from disappointment, we desire relief from the pain, and we are the most vulnerable to temptation, assault, deception, and accusation from the enemy. He intensely bombards us with his tools of destruction. However, it is also during our disappointments that we have the opportunity to press into God and cling to His promises. In these trials we have the occasion to become more Christlike; we can grow and gain strength in ways that we would not otherwise. And in our distress, most importantly, we get to know God in a deeper way (see Job 42:1-6).

Please understand that God is not the one who brings disappointment. He never brings about or tempts us with evil. We have pain because we live in a world full of trouble. Jesus prayed that God would protect us from the evil one (see John 17:15), not take us out of the world. We can pray in agreement with Jesus to be protected from the enemy and the effect of his assaults. Disappointment does not have to make your heart sick.

GUARD YOUR HEART

One of the most important scriptures in the Bible is found in Proverbs 4:23, "Guard your heart above all else, for it determines the course of your life" (NLT). We must not allow anything contrary to the Word and nature of God to enter our hearts. As soon as disappointment comes into our life, we must go to God *immediately*. This guards against the enemy's attempts to plant his venom in our hearts. If he succeeds in planting those poisonous seeds, the fruit will manifest and bring destruction to our lives.

"Guard your heart above all else, for it determines the course of your life" (Proverbs 4:23 NLT). As soon as disappointment comes into our life, we must go to God immediately. This guards against the enemy's attempts to plant his venom in our hearts.

Let's look at some biblical examples of destructive fruit, and as we do, ask the Holy Spirit to highlight any area in your heart that He wants to heal. Let the healing process begin with the awareness that He brings.

FRUIT OF A SICK HEART

SUSPICION

Suspicion is the inability to trust. When our hearts are wounded, this is one of the first signs to manifest. If the wound is left unhealed, the enemy causes us to build a wall around our heart, which seals in the pain and keeps out God's healing love.

In 1 Samuel 18, David had just returned from a successful battle campaign, and the people were praising him more than Saul. The disappointment within Saul's heart caused him to be suspicious of David from that day forward (see 1 Samuel 18:9 NAS). Saul's heart became so consumed with distrust that he spent the next several years trying to kill David. From this example, we can see how important it is to guard our hearts against anything that differs from how God feels.

The inability to trust will make it a struggle to maintain healthy relationships. While we may not go as far as Saul did against David, we *will* miss out on the blessing of thriving relationships.

SKEPTICISM & CYNICISM

Skepticism and cynicism take suspicion to the next level. While skepticism is a display of mistrust, cynicism means to be bitterly or sneeringly distrustful, contemptuous, or pessimistic. Gideon and Zacharias (John the Baptist's father) are two glaring examples. The Lord Himself approached Gideon, and an angel visited Zacharias – yet they both responded in skepticism.

Gideon's response also revealed a measure of cynicism. His response was "If the Lord is with us, why then has all this happened to us? And where are all His miracles which our fathers told us about?" (Judges 6:13). His disappointment with life had accumulated to the point of doubting God.

Zacharias was old and without child, and when the prophetic promise came, he was skeptical, unable to believe due to years of failed expectations. An unhealed heart that manifests the fruits of skepticism and cynicism will keep us from receiving the promises and word of God when it comes.

RESENTMENT

Resentment is displeasure or indignation over some act, remark, person, etc., which you feel caused injury or insult. It is one of the subtlest assaults of the enemy because many times, the seed is sown in our hearts without any awareness of it. Though resentment usually starts in small ways, it will ultimately grow and lead to other destructive patterns. Often, by the time it is recognized it has developed into self-destructive mindsets that consume our souls.

Resentment will always lead to despising if it is not exposed and healed. King David's wife, Michal, despised David in her heart when she saw him dance before the Lord (see 1 Chronicles 15:29 NKJV). We know that Michal loved David – she had even previously saved his life from her father, Saul (see 1 Samuel 19:11-18).

Surely she knew that David was a lover and worshipper of God. What happened that caused her to resent and despise David? When David was running for his life from Saul, Michal was given to another man (1 Samuel 25:44). Perhaps Michal was devastated that David did not rescue her from this other man, especially after she had saved David's life. Because of her unhealed heart through that disappointment, her resentment grew to the place where she despised him.

SELF-PITY

Self-pity is a self-indulgent attitude concerning one's own difficulties and hardships. It is one of the most destructive fruits of a sick heart. A good friend once said, "Self-pity is a deep ditch; the longer you stay in it, the harder it is to get out." That is so true.

One reason it becomes difficult to get out of self-pity is that it actually begins to feel good! Some become so familiar with it that they don't want to let it go. Self-pity relieves us from any responsibility and places blame on others and circumstances. Instead of taking responsibility, the attitude of entitlement dominates us to the degree that we can begin to live as if the whole world owes us something. However, the damaging result is a life lived in despair and hopelessness.

The man with an infirmity for thirty-eight years in John 5 is a prime example of self-pity. When Jesus approached him and asked if he wanted to get well, he responded, "No one will ever help me and everybody else always beats me" (paraphrased). This is a classic response of self-pity and blame. Years of disappointment had left the man in despair and hopelessness.

HOPELESSNESS & UNBELIEF

These fruits are just a sample of many more. However, *all* of them lead to hopelessness and unbelief. A heart without hope is a sick heart. Of course, there are varying degrees of hopelessness, but anyone without hope struggles daily to find a purpose to live. The good news is that God is the restorer of hope. Jesus came to give us life and to give it to us *abundantly*!

A few years ago, we did an outreach in the inner city where a large population of homeless people lived. We struck up a conversation with a man who, like so many of the homeless, was angry, bitter, and without hope. At first he was aggressive in his speech, but as we shared with him the love of God, his countenance slowly began to change. By the end of the conversation he had tears running down his face. He gave me a hug and said, "Thank you all. *I now have hope again.*" That is what our God does. It is His supernatural love and goodness that brings hope and faith back into a wounded heart and life.

If you are in a state of hopelessness now, I want to encourage you. "It is too late" is the common lie of hopelessness, but, as long as there is breath in your body, you are a candidate for the love, hope, and faith of God! I pray for you now, may "The God of hope fill you with all joy and peace in believing, **that you may abound in hope** by the power of the Holy Spirit" (Romans 15:13, emphasis added).

KEYS TO HEAL THE SICK HEART

HONESTY/TRANSPARENCY

> Behold, You desire truth in the inward parts, and in the hidden part You will make me to know wisdom. — Psalm 51:6 NAS

Always, the first step to any healing is to get honest. Do not put it off! Get honest with yourself. Get honest with God. At all cost, avoid the pit of denial. Though opening your heart can be painful, it is the only way to receive God's love and healing.

We see from Psalm 51:6 that we receive needed insight and wisdom by opening those hidden places we have kept walled off. Pray the prayer of the psalmist when he said, "Search me and know my heart. Try me, and know my anxieties" (Psalm 139:23). When you close your heart to God, it opens your heart to the enemy.

REPENTANCE

As you open your heart, be ready and willing to agree with God. Repentance is the key that positions us to receive everything God has provided. Refusal to repent is really nothing more than justifying your own actions or choices. It is pride.

Have you ever considered the foolishness of arguing with God? If God calls something sin, then it is sin. When God exposes wrong attitudes or beliefs it is always for our good. Many times we stay locked in a worldly repentance, which is being sorry for being caught, instead of godly

We receive needed insight and wisdom by opening those hidden places we have kept walled off. Pray the prayer of the psalmist when he said, "Search me and know my heart. Try me, and know my anxieties" (Psalm 139:23).

repentance, which is sorrow for the act. Worldly repentance often places blame on others; it is a form of self-protection, which leads to death. Self–protection is rooted in fear and often deceives us. It is such a lie! But godly sorrow leads to repentance, which brings life and freedom (see 2 Corinthians 7:8-10).

We are all familiar with the sufferings of Job. At first he is the perfect model, giving God honor in the midst of everything. But finally he has had too much and lashes out at God, who lovingly but very firmly proceeds to remind Job of who He is. This revelation leads Job into repentance; he humbles himself and declares: "I had only heard about you before, but now I have seen you with my own eyes. I take back everything I said, and I sit in dust and ashes to show my repentance" (Job 42:5-6). Job's heart adjustment paved the way for God to heal and restore him.

To the degree that we abandon ourselves to God and let go of self-protection is the degree that we open our heart and position ourselves for His healing. God's loving correction is always filled with hope, even if it is painful initially (see Hebrews 12:5-11).

FORGIVENESS

So many times we try and have the right emotions to forgive. They seldom – if ever – come. We MUST make the *choice* to forgive. The emotions will come as God heals our hearts. Unforgiveness probably keeps more people – believers and unbelievers alike – in bondage than anything else. Its fruit of bitterness destroys peoples' joy, health, and relationships.

When you determine that the value of the person who wronged you is greater than the debt they owe you, you can forgive. Jesus values them greatly and gave everything for them – "Who for the joy set before Him, endured the cross, despising the shame" (Hebrews 12:2). You can despise the wrong done and at the same time choose the joy of knowing the offender has been valued by Jesus through His payment for them on the cross. Choose to forgive!

When I finished a nine-month ministry school in 1990, the president of the school made the statement, "If you leave here and can't repent or forgive, then we can't help you." Wow! That is so true and it still impacts my life today.

FEAR OF THE LORD

The fear of the Lord is to hate evil (Proverbs 8:13 KJV). By mercy and truth, iniquity is purged, and by the fear of the Lord, men depart from evil (Proverbs 16:6 KJV). Jesus told His disciples that the only thing they were to fear was God (Matthew 10:28). To fear the Lord is to know that He is the only source in which we can confidently place our hope and trust.

When we truly come to an understanding of the destructive nature of sin, we fear stepping out from under the protection of God. Yes, we need a reverential fear of the Lord, which causes us to tremble at His presence and power. There are many examples in the Bible of men falling prostrate before the Lord in this kind of fear. But when we couple this with a true knowledge of His love for us, the fear of the Lord becomes a desire in our heart. The enemy tries to place a fear of the Lord on us that causes us to avoid God. But true fear of the Lord will cause us to long for Him and draw near to Him.

Fear of the Lord includes a hatred for unbelief. There are several examples in the life of Jesus where He would be grieved when He encountered unbelief (see Matthew 17:17, Mark 16:14). Years ago, I asked the Lord, "Why is unbelief so bad?" and He responded, "When you don't believe Me, you are doubting the nature of My love for you."

Let's ask for and receive from God a fresh revelation and impartation of the fear of the Lord!

SACRIFICE OF PRAISE

Offering the sacrifice of praise is one of the most powerful weapons we have. When we choose to praise God in the midst of disappointment, we position ourselves for Him to work on our behalf. Praising God for who He is in the midst of pain is the ultimate statement of faith. He is the Lord God. He does not change (Malachi. 3:2, Lamentations 3:22). He is worthy of praise all the time. In the world, this might be considered hypocrisy. But in the kingdom of God, it is a wonderful display, which brings pleasure to the heart of God.

> Praising God for who He is in the midst of pain is the ultimate statement of faith. He is the Lord God. He is worthy of praise all the time.

Surely, one of the most poignant incidents in the Bible is when David fights for the life of his newborn. The prophet Nathan has already warned him that the child, the fruit of David's sin, will die. David sincerely repents but, even so, the baby becomes deathly ill. For seven days, David goes without food and lies on the bare ground pleading with God for his child's life, but... the baby dies. As soon as he finds out, David gets up, washes himself, and goes straight to the tabernacle to worship God. That sounds like a sacrifice of praise to me! Undoubtedly, that act of abandoned worship helps David get out of his "funk." He is soon able to carry out all of his kingly duties again and sometime after, he and Bathsheba conceive again, and Solomon is born.

I encourage you to praise Him with all your being. Don't just think it; do something! Shout. Sing. Dance. Declare His Word. Praise Him!

THE HEALED HEART

As we go into the next chapters, which deal with specific areas of disappointment, apply these tools of truth and allow the Holy Spirit to touch your heart. Do not be in a hurry or simply look for more information. **Information alone will not heal. It is the revelation of God's love and truth deep in your heart that heals.** Take time to let God work in your soul – let Him expose the lies. Let Him bring truth and heal (Jeremiah 17:14). Let Him restore hope and faith. Let Him place a fiery passion back in your life for the remembrance of His name (Isaiah 26:8). Let Him give you an intimate relationship with the Father, Son, and Holy Spirit like you have never experienced.

These are words that I have often sung and prayed in times of pain and disappointment:

> I kneel before you Father, in the shadow of Your might.
>
> And I pray that You will hear this cry, and heal this heart tonight.
>
> I'm longing for You, Lord. I need You to fill me more and more.
>
> I'm desperate for You, Jesus. Whatever You have to do, make me more like You.
>
> May the scars I bear be sacred, and this brokenness be real.
>
> May the wounds so deep inside my heart, reflect You as they heal.
>
> — "More Like You" by Kim Hill

Are you ready? He is there for you!

HEART CHECK-UP

1. What is your expectation level?

2. Do you recognize some of the fruit of an unhealed heart in your own life?

3. Have the keys to a healed heart helped you overcome in the past? Are there some areas in which you need to apply one or more of these keys again? Which ones?

PRAYER

Father, I recognize that my expectations for abundant life are lower than what You have promised. I invite Your Spirit to search me and reveal the places I have allowed unbelief to enter my heart. Show me any lies in which I have come into agreement, and I will renounce them! I open my heart You; I will receive and believe Your TRUTH and hold fast to Your words in the midst of my circumstances. I proclaim that You are faithful and good, and far greater than anything I face! I will allow my expectations to align with Your goodness and Your promises!

2

DISAPPOINTMENT WITH GOD

TIM WAS THE YOUNGEST of four children and only two years old when his father left the family. He began to ride the church bus to Sunday school when he was seven, and he was immediately drawn to the loving atmosphere. His childlike faith was stirred when the teacher said that he could ask Jesus for anything and He would answer, so Tim began to ask Jesus to bring his father back to their family. He was full of faith, expectation, and hope. Days turned into weeks. Weeks turned into months, and months into years. His father never returned to the family. By the time Tim was a teenager, he had lost hope, and he stopped asking.

Can you relate? Who of us has not doubted God in our heart at some point? The truth is that most of our disappointments are rooted in a belief that God has failed us. But this can be hard to recognize or acknowledge and as a result, we are prone to focus our issues toward others. But in the depths of our hearts there are beliefs that beg the questions: How could God let this happen? After all, isn't He sovereign? We seldom acknowledge these types of thoughts because they contradict the belief that God is always perfect and good. Therefore, the very notion of being disappointed with God places us in a paradoxical position. How can you be disappointed with someone who is perfect?

Resolving this heart issue first requires that we become transparent and honest with *ourselves*. God already knows what is in our hearts. **In truth, every disappointment we deal with will ultimately pertain to our relationship with God.** Our approach to each area of disappointment will be based upon our perspective of Him. In other words, how we see God in each situation will determine the true condition of our hearts and what we really believe (see Proverbs 23:7). If we believe that God has let us down, then our hearts will become sick with disappointment and vulnerable to the assault of hopelessness. Many then develop erroneous theology in order to bring resolve to their heart, which is really a heart full of unbelief and wrong mindsets about the goodness of God and who He really is.

THE WRONG QUESTIONS

> And His disciples asked Him, saying, "Rabbi, who sinned, this man or his parents, that he was born blind?"
>
> Jesus answered, "Neither this man nor his parents sinned, but that the works of God should be revealed in him. I must work the works of Him who sent Me while it is day; the night is coming when no one can work.
>
> — John 9:2-4

In this verse, the disciples asked Jesus who was to blame for a man being born blind. The first consideration was senseless. To even consider the possibility that the blind man sinned before he was born reveals the deception we fall into when we try to explain what we don't understand (more on this later).

Next, to consider that God would inflict blindness upon a child because of a parent's sin is to reveal a belief contrary to who God really is. Are you kidding me? A good God would inflict suffering upon an innocent child to punish his parents? Absurd!

In verse three, Jesus reveals the kingdom purposes of God in this situation. His answer is simple and to the point, "Neither this man nor his parents sinned." Many theologians teach that Jesus' next statement, "that the works of God should be revealed in him," meant that God made the man blind in order to reveal the works of God in his healing. This is equally absurd. A good God would never create evil in order to prove that He is good or to show His power.

Jesus was basically telling them, "Your focus is in the wrong place. Your questions reveal that what you believe about God and why I am here is wrong. You need only to know that I am here now to do the works of God, and in this situation, the work of God is to heal this blind man." And that is what He did!

Jesus was saying to His disciples that He was here to destroy all of the works of the devil (1 John 3:8). Yes, there is evil in the world. Yes, sin entered upon man's choice to disobey God. But all of the suffering in this world is the result of the works of satan. God forgive us when we blame Him for evil and suffering!

Our enemy knows that when we are rooted and grounded in the revelation of who God is and His love for us, we are unshakable. That is why he seeks every possible opportunity to assault the character of God. When he succeeds in planting those seeds of doubt in our hearts, our very faith is at risk. Let's go back and look at the strategy of the enemy from the beginning.

DID GOD REALLY SAY?

The Bible gives us our first introduction to satan in Genesis 3. In verse 1, his character is immediately exposed. He is cunning! The first words we hear out of his mouth are, "Did God really say?" (NIV). The first lesson here is obvious: we must know what God has said. The only way to ever engage the enemy in conversation is with an authoritative address with the true Word of God (see Matthew 4:1-10).

But in this case, Eve opened herself up to the accusation of satan against the character of God. Through subtle deception and cunning insinuation, satan was able to bring confusion to Eve. In Genesis 3:3, we find her misquoting God as having said they could not even *touch* the tree of the knowledge of good and evil. While it may seem a small thing, it underscores the importance of the Word of God. Any misunderstanding of God's Word opens us up to a misguided belief system. In verse 5, we find the lie that satan was sowing: "God knows that when you eat [from the tree of knowledge] you will be like Him." In other words, God is holding out on you. He is not really completely good or trustworthy!

How many times have you heard someone say, "If God is so good, then why…?" The list to fill in this blank is almost endless. It's not surprising that this accusation works against unbelievers. Their minds are blinded (2 Corinthians 4:4), but for believers, it should not be so.

When believers receive that seed of doubt (i.e. that accusation against the goodness of God), it leaves them in a crisis of faith. First, we must realize that the possibility for this exists within each one of us. If satan was able to successfully plant this seed in Eve, who was walking in pure, unbroken fellowship with God, then certainly it exists within us who are in the process of being sanctified.

Next, we must position ourselves to allow God's truth to examine our hearts in order to bring the healing we so desperately need. We must let go of our erroneous perceptions of God and believe He is, indeed, who He says He is!

I want to emphasize a very important truth: we should never have more fear of the enemy's ability to deceive us than God's ability to preserve, protect, and keep us in the truth (see Jude 24). Jesus promised that the Holy Spirit will guide us into all truth (John 16:8)! Being aware of the enemy's strategy is primarily needed to keep us aware of our dependence upon God. Eve's mistake of conversing with

---

We should never have more fear of the enemy's ability to deceive us than God's ability to preserve, protect, and keep us in the truth: "[He] is able to keep you from stumbling and to present you before his glorious presence without fault and with great joy" (Jude 24).

---

satan shifted her focus away from God. As we stay near to Him, we can trust that He will stay near to us and protect us from the schemes of the evil one.

Now let's look at ways we are vulnerable to receive the enemy's seeds. There are two aspects of disappointment with God. The first has to do with unmet expectations and the second has to do with the mysteries of God.

UNMET EXPECTATIONS

When Karen's marriage was failing, she met an inspiring Christian woman who encouraged her to write a list of Bible promises that reflected what she wanted to happen in her marriage, and to declare them every day. She explained that this was a powerful tool to increase and activate faith, and see miracles happen. Karen was excited and hopeful. Even though she was already a strong Christian, this was the first time she had heard about this powerful weapon. Karen meticulously wrote out a number of biblical promises and decreed them several times of day. Her faith began to grow, and she was even more encouraged when she heard testimonies of others whose marriages or other impossible situations had been overcome in this manner. Full of faith, Karen even set a specific date that she believed her marriage would be restored. But when that day arrived, the opposite happened: she discovered clear evidence that her husband was having an affair.

Devastated and angry, she threw the sheets of decrees across the room, crying out to God, "What good is your Word if Your promises are for everyone but me?"

Remember, the stronghold of unbelief is sown in the seed of disappointment. All disappointments are a result of unmet expectations. If I have learned anything in life, it is that things simply don't always turn out like we think they will. This can be reconciled when we deal with others, because we understand that no one is perfect. But when dealing with God, it's harder to accept our unmet expectations. If God is perfect, then how can we be disappointed? How can He not meet our expectations? The answers to these questions position us to come into a true place of healing within our hearts.

MISGUIDED & UNREALISTIC EXPECTATIONS

Misguided and unrealistic expectations always leave us vulnerable to disappointment. Every expectation we have of God must be rooted in His revealed will and Word. When we receive a promise from God, we are prone to add our interpretation of how that promise will manifest. **Our expectations are based on what *we* desire His promises to look like for us.**

The injection of our soul's desires dilutes the pure promises of God. Our soul can even desire good things like healing, deliverance, etc., but when soulish desire masks itself as faith, it is actually presumption. When our expectations are based upon our desires, apart from a clear understanding of God's promises or His will in a situation, it is a sure setup for disappointment.

The greatest biblical example of this is found in the life of John the Baptist. No one received greater revelation and promise concerning the Messiah than John. John knew his identity scripturally (see Isaiah 40:3, Malachi 3:1) and by prophetic revelation. God also told John how he would recognize the Messiah (John 1:33), and that promise was fulfilled when John actually saw the Spirit of God descend upon Jesus (John 1:32). He declared in John 1:34 that Jesus was the Son of God, and, later, that Jesus must increase but he must decrease. But what did that mean, and what did *John* think it meant?

After John the Baptist was thrown in prison, he began to doubt that Jesus was even the Messiah. How could he possibly doubt after he received so much revelation and promise? We can only speculate as to all of John's thoughts, but I doubt prison was in his interpretation of the prophetic promises he had received. Maybe he imagined walking side by side with Jesus, serving with Him for the rest of his life, or perhaps he envisioned a continued ministry of going to various places and "preparing the way" for Jesus.

Can you imagine the thoughts and accusations of the enemy? "John, you gave your entire life to serve God and prepare the way for the Messiah and now He leaves you in prison? He doesn't even come visit you! What kind of God do you serve?" Sound familiar? Whatever John's thoughts were, we can be sure that in his disappointment, the enemy was there to viciously assault him and bring him to a place of despair and unbelief.

The lesson for us to learn is clear: every revelation and promise we receive from God, including scriptural promises, must not be tainted with our interpretations and desires.

One of the greatest insights I have learned from Patricia King is that there are three parts to every prophetic word and promise: revelation, interpretation, and application. What did God say? What did He mean? What does He want me to do with it?

I believe interpretation is one of the most neglected aspects to this principle. When we fail to truly understand what God means when He speaks, we will be vulnerable to disappointment. This is not about persevering until the promise comes – we know that every promise will be tested (Psalm 105:19), and we should always be strong in faith until the promise comes (see Romans 4:17-21). I'm addressing promises to which we have added our own interpretations and expectations and as a result, we are setup for disappointment.

Many think that Jesus should have at least visited John in prison and given him some explanation. After all, was not Jesus the One who came to set the captives free? But remember, Jesus said to tell John that the blind see and the

There are three parts to every prophetic word and promise: revelation, interpretation, and application. When we fail to truly understand what God means when He speaks, we will be vulnerable to disappointment.

lame walk; the lepers are cleansed and the deaf hear. The dead are raised up and the poor have the gospel preached to them (Matthew 11:4-5). Jesus did not tell John anything that he did not already know. Jesus was reassuring John that He was who John had believed Him to be; He was all that he had believed for and so much more! Though things were not turning out like John had expected, Jesus was strengthening his heart with reassurance.

Finally, Jesus said to tell John, "Blessed is he who is not offended because of me" (Matthew 11:6). This was not a rebuke – it was Jesus encouraging the prophet to not let the enemy cause him to stumble in his faith. He wants to encourage you as well! Don't let the enemy feed you his lies that undermine your faith and hope. He knows how powerful you are against the works of darkness when you are strong in faith.

Don't allow the enemy to cause you to accuse God. We should always draw near to God in our trials and cry out to Him for understanding. However, we must make the distinction between demanding an explanation and asking for understanding. To *demand an explanation* is to elevate yourself above God, but when you *ask for understanding*, you've positioned yourself to know Him in a deeper and more intimate way. It was from this humble position that the Apostle Paul said he suffered the loss of all things and counted them as dung that he may not only gain Christ, but ultimately know Him (see Philippians 3:1-10)!

Remember Karen? She shares that after her outburst, God spoke to her tenderly. He did not tell her He would fulfill her expectations, but instead, invited her to get to know Him better and form a deeper relationship with Him. "His voice was so full of love that in that moment, I knew I wanted to learn how to love Him better more than anything, no matter what the future held." Ultimately, her marriage did end but by then, Karen's faith in her loving God was rock solid, and her vibrant relationship with Him helped her to quickly heal and move on.

Maybe you are confused about a promise God has made (or you believe He has made) to you, or perhaps you have had so many disappointments that you are in a place of hopelessness and unbelief. Remember, God is good. He longs to strengthen your heart and restore your hope. Take time now with God, and ask Him to reveal Himself to you afresh. Ask Him to silence the voice of the enemy, and allow Him to gently reveal where you may have added your own interpretations to His promises. He is the Spirit of Truth!

THE MYSTERIES OF GOD

At times, the unexplainable is simply due to our lack of understanding, but there are also times when the unexplainable lies within the mysteries of God. Deuteronomy 29:29 says, "Secret things belong to the Lord our God, but the things revealed belong to us and to our children forever" (NAS).

God never promised that we would have the answers to all of our questions in this life, but rather that we only know "in part" (see 1 Corinthians 13:9). He is Lord, and He is God – we must be prepared to live with His unexplainable mysteries without being disappointed in Him. More importantly, we must not become offended at God.

Undoubtedly, there are unanswered questions: Why are some supernaturally healed, but others aren't? Why did God "allow" the accident that snatched the life of that young person in the prime of their lives? Why has injustice been allowed to prevail, wrecking lives and livelihoods? These questions particularly hit home when it has to do with someone we deeply love or admire.

With a peaceful heart, we must accept the truth that there are questions and circumstances that will be unexplainable and unanswerable, but we do not need to make excuses for God or make up an answer in order to have one. There's no need to pull back from aggressive faith in God and His promises!

A passive acceptance of trials that we relegate to "simply being the will of God" is really an excuse for our unbelief. For every circumstance that *seems* contrary to the will of God, the wise choice on our part is to offer no explanation. That is God's business. If *He* doesn't explain, then neither should we! Every effort to do so will most likely result in error and pride. The psalmist said it this way,

> Lord, my heart is not haughty, nor my eyes lofty. Neither do I concern myself with great matters, nor with things too profound for me. Surely I have calmed and quieted my soul. Like a weaned child with his mother. Like a weaned child is my soul within me. O Israel, hope in the Lord from this time forth and forever. — Psalm 131

KEY TRUTHS TO REMEMBER

Let's look at some key truths, which will keep us from being offended at God in the midst of what we don't understand.

FAITH VS. TRUST

Faith is a real substance that we possess (see Hebrews 11:1). In its purest form, it is taking God at His Word. Faith is conceived and birthed out of the promises of God.

Trust, in its purest form, maintains the viewpoint of God's goodness when circumstances don't seem to align with our understanding of His promises. Our trust must be rooted in the truth of God's character coupled with His revealed Word.

If we only have His Word without an unshakeable confidence in who He is, then all we have is information, even though it be truth. If you do not trust a person who speaks to you, then you will not believe what he says. It is the same with God. Trust is a foundational belief in God's goodness in the midst of the unexplainable.

People often believe they need more faith when what they really need is to have their heart healed concerning their belief in the goodness of God. Great faith in the revealed Word of God is absolutely necessary, but ultimately, it is your trust in who He is that will prepare your heart to receive that Word.

A great example of this kind of trust is in Matthew 15:21-28 – a Gentile woman approached Jesus with a desperate plea for Him to heal her daughter. When Jesus told her it was not right to give the children's bread to dogs, she responded with a statement that revealed her heart and who she believed Jesus to be. No doubt she had heard a multitude

People often believe they need more faith when what they really need is to have their heart healed concerning their belief in the goodness of God.

of stories about the wonderful miracles Jesus had performed, and possibly, she had even witnessed some of them. Her response revealed a confidence based in His goodness, and that had prepared her heart to believe what He would do for her daughter. Yes, her faith was great, but it was her confidence that she would not be rejected by Him, because of His goodness, that gave her boldness to even ask.

When we base our trust on *our understanding of God and His promises,* we open ourselves to deception, confusion, and ultimately disappointment. When we base our trust on *the nature and character of God,* then we open ourselves to abundant life and peace that passes understanding.

As we live in this place of trust, we will continue to grow in the knowledge of who He is. The more we remain in faith concerning the goodness of God, the more we will be prone to believe that He will do what He says, and this positions us to see His promises manifest in our lives.

Several years ago, I was dealing with the effects of a huge disappointment. At the time, everything was going well in my life and yet I was constantly aware of how little passion I had for God and the things of God. I honestly did not understand why – I had done all I knew to do. I had repented. I had forgiven. I had asked for forgiveness and blessed those who did not forgive me. I had broken word curses.... You get the picture.

One day, as I was reading the following Scripture, the Lord opened my heart wide.

> Therefore thus says the Lord [to Jeremiah]: If you return **[and give up this mistaken tone of distrust and despair]**, then I will give you again a settled place of quiet and safety, and you will be My minister; and if you separate the precious from the vile **[cleansing your own heart from unworthy and unwarranted suspicions concerning God's faithfulness]**, you shall be My mouthpiece.
>
> — Jeremiah 15:19 AMP
> (emphasis added)

It was as if God inserted my name in the place of Jeremiah's. The Lord showed me that the problem was not past disappointments with people or circumstances. Rather, my heart had received a seed from the enemy, which had blossomed into unbelief. I was in distrust, despair, and even suspicion about the faithfulness of God. OUCH!

My heart was so grieved that I began to weep. Holy Spirit then asked me to read Psalm 89 and I saw that "Your faithfulness" appeared four times in the first eight verses. I said to God, "I get it: You are faithful. You are good." As painful as it was, it was also one of the most liberating moments in my life. I am so thankful that God loves me enough to expose and heal my heart.

THE CROSS

The foundation for every believer's trust in the goodness of God must be rooted in the revelation of the cross. I'm concerned that sometimes we are so familiar with the story of the cross that we lose the impact of God's love displayed there. The sacrificial death of Jesus on the cross is certainly the basis of our redemption, but so much more! More than anything, it is the most amazing display of love ever demonstrated in all of humanity. "Greater love has no man than this, than he lay down his life for his friends" was Jesus' declaration about His sacrificial death for us. The ultimate in unbelief is to look at the cross and yet not believe that God loves us.

Years ago, I visited a young woman in a psychiatric ward who had just attempted suicide for the fourth time. I tried everything I knew to comfort and encourage her, but I was acutely aware that there was no impact or progress being made because a strong spirit of self-pity was working in her. I silently prayed for her and asked God for wisdom, and He led me to ask her a series of questions. I said, "Do you believe in Jesus? Do you believe that He was beaten, and He suffered, and that He died on the cross for you? Do you believe that He rose from the dead?"

She answered yes to all the questions. Then I said, "And was that not enough for you?" This was not an attempt

If you struggle to feel loved by God, stop now and ask for a fresh revelation of the cross. Ask Him to open the eyes of your heart, and then step out in faith – begin to praise Him for His great display of love for you on the cross.

to manipulate with guilt, but to bring reality into focus. The atmosphere changed immediately – her countenance changed, and the ugly spirit of self-pity and unbelief was exposed. The reality of Jesus' death on the cross came into full revelation. How we need a fresh revelation of His great love for us, which was demonstrated on the cross!

If you struggle to feel loved by God, stop now and ask for a fresh revelation of the cross. Ask Him to open the eyes of your heart, and then step out in faith – begin to praise Him for His great display of love for you on the cross.

You will be able to filter through the voices of darkness, which come against you, only as the meaning of the cross becomes central to your life. Then, unbelief and hopelessness will lose their grip on your life, and you will begin to experience the fullness of His love – your life will be transformed (see Ephesians 3:19 NLT)! I pray that the revelation of the cross will penetrate your entire being in a new and fresh way and that you will experience the power of His love like never before!

RIGHTEOUSNESS & JUSTICE

When we understand God's righteousness and justice, it helps tremendously with the question of "How could God let this happen?" Righteousness and justice are the foundation of God's throne, and all the paths of the Lord are mercy and truth (Psalm 89:14 & 25:10). The ability of God to execute righteousness and justice and demonstrate mercy at the same time, can only be understood through the power of the cross. This is why Paul said that through God's wisdom in proclaiming the message of the cross, the power of the cross would accomplish His purposes (1 Corinthians 1:18, 21).

The cross not only displayed His great love, but it also satisfied the need for justice while remaining merciful. Through the cross, God remained faithful to His nature – He displayed righteousness and executed justice against sin. At the same time, He accomplished the greatest desire of His heart – He showed mercy to all of mankind and restored them to a loving relationship with Himself. By the sacrifice of Jesus on the cross, God was able to display His hatred for sin and His love for humanity at the same time!

Many people have shared with me how that when they were children, they cried out to God for help and He did not answer. The following is a story from a dear friend of mine, which beautifully illustrates the righteousness, justice, and mercy of God. As you read, think about this truth: if God released His righteousness and justice upon mankind without mercy, there would be no one left. We would all be consumed.

THE WRATH OF GOD SPARED

While sitting on the couch in the counseling office of a skilled and trusted Christian counselor, I began to share about a specific painful memory of being sexually abused at the age of eight by my stepfather. Over the years, I carried shame, anger, and the relentless need to know why God would allow something like this to happen. This day provided an answer I never expected.

With the gentle guidance of my counselor, I agreed to close my eyes, reflect on that day, and ask Jesus to show me where He was. Immediately, as if I were vividly reliving the event all over again, I recalled being grabbed and thrust to the floor under the force and weight of my stepfather's body. However, this time, instead of having my eyes closed and wishing I could disappear, I opened my eyes.

I looked around and to my surprise, Jesus stood at the feet of my stepfather. In that moment, I became aware of only Him. He was dressed in a white robe with His back turned toward us. His arms were outstretched from His sides, as if to hide the shame of what was taking place. Next to the sleeves that draped down to His wrists, I could see the visible scars on His hands from the nails that held Him to the cross.

I heard the voice of the counselor break in and ask if I could see Jesus there. Overwhelmed by what I saw and felt, I could only shake my head affirming that He was there. I then heard the question, "What is He doing?"

Instantly, my thoughts raced back to the images of where He stood. Anger rose up – I was helpless and powerless to stop what was taking place – I heard myself cry out, "Why are You just standing there? WHY DON'T YOU DO SOMETHING?"

He turned His head toward His left shoulder so His words could easily be heard; yet He was careful not to look upon what was happening. Large tears rolled down His cheek, and His expression conveyed great sadness, anger, and compassion all at once. He replied, "I am doing something. I am reminding the Father of the price I paid to spare this man from the wrath of God. He created man with a free will and will not violate the free will He created, even though man violates God's will. It was not God's will for this to happen and it grieves and angers Him to the point of wrath. But I died that he may be forgiven and that you may be healed of the effects of this man's sin. As a child you could not understand but today, as My child, you can."

I could no longer hold back the tears; I was overcome with a tremendous sense of love that flooded my heart like I had never felt before. The counselor asked how I was doing and if I thought

I could continue. I told her I was okay and willing to go on.

She asked what happened after my stepfather finished having his way with me. I explained how he would threaten to kill mother, my brothers, and me if I told anyone what had happened. He often slapped me while shouting, "Do you understand?"

Sobbing and cowering in fear I would reply, "Yes, I promise; I won't tell." He would then command that I stop crying and go to my room until my mother returned home. I would retreat to my room where, in pain, I curled up on my bed in a fetal position and silently cried myself to sleep.

The counselor suggested that I do as I did previously: invite Jesus to meet me once again in that place. I consented, closed my eyes, and asked Him where He was.

I was instantly in the moment when I was walking back to my room. This time I stopped in the doorway, amazed to see Jesus sitting on the side of my bed as if He had been expecting me. He looked at me with eyes that showed so much love and compassion.

He stretched His right hand toward me, inviting me to join Him. I just stared at Him, afraid to be touched yet longing to feel safe and protected. I hesitantly approached and dared to take His hand. Ever so gently, He drew me near then positioned me on His lap, wrapped me in His arms, and silently rocked me.

This went on for several minutes before He laid me on the bed and comforted me in a quiet, reassuring tone, "It's going to be okay." His love dissolved all my fear.

I opened my eyes and tears ran down my face as I once again took in the surroundings of the counselor's office. I was overwhelmed with incredible relief in my heart, calmness in my soul, and quiet peace of mind.

We ended that session in prayer, thanksgiving, and joy for what God did in one hour that otherwise may have taken months, even years, to accomplish.

What an amazing story! "Oh, the depth of the riches both of the wisdom and knowledge of God! How unsearchable are His judgments and His ways past finding out" (Romans 11:33 NKJV)!

Meditate on this passage from Romans; it is one of the most encouraging passages in Scripture.

Therefore, since we are justified (acquitted, declared righteous, and given a right standing with God) through faith, let us [grasp the fact that we] have [the peace of reconciliation to hold and to enjoy] peace with God through our Lord Jesus Christ (the Messiah, the Anointed One).

Through Him also we have [our] access (entrance, introduction) by faith into this grace (state of God's favor) in which we [firmly and safely] stand. And let us rejoice and exult in our hope of experiencing and enjoying the glory of God.

Moreover [let us also be full of joy now!] let us exult and triumph in our troubles and rejoice in our sufferings, knowing that pressure and affliction and hardship produce patient and unswerving endurance.

And endurance (fortitude) develops maturity of character (approved faith and tried integrity). And character [of this sort] produces [the habit of] joyful and confident hope of eternal salvation.

Such hope never disappoints or deludes or shames us, for God's love has been poured out in our hearts through the Holy Spirit Who has been given to us.

— Romans 5:1-5

Because of our standing with God, we have the joy of experiencing and enjoying His glory. We can be full of joy even when trials are upon us – our endurance is strengthened; our character is proven, and our hope is increased! Such hope never disappoints, because it is the love of God, which is revealed by the Holy Spirit. I pray for you now to encounter a fresh baptism of His love!

HEART CHECK-UP

1. Have there been times that you expected God to do something, and it didn't turn out the way you wanted?

2. What did you do with that disappointment? Did you push it aside, but it still lurks in your heart? Or did you press in to God, and ask Him to reveal Himself to you in a deeper way?

3. Are there any steps you need to take to address some unresolved issues in your heart? What are they?

PRAYER

Lord, You are my Light and my Life, and I desire to know You MORE! Please reveal Yourself to me in a deeper way than what I have known. I want to SEE You not just hear of You. Give me eyes to see beyond just what's in front of me. Give me eyes that see only You. Invade every part of me with Your Spirit and sweep out any doubts that have lurked in my heart, regarding Your faithfulness or Your love toward me. You are my God, and I place my trust and my faith in You: my Rock, my Joy, and my Love.

3

DISAPPOINTMENT WITH SELF

S ECOND TO HIS ASSAULT on the goodness and character
of God is the enemy's constant barrage of accusation
against the believer in the midst of their own shortcomings.

Very few understand disappointment with self like those
who struggle with addiction. I first met Sarah over fifteen
years ago. She was raised in a loving, stable home but as a
young teenager, she gave in to the constant assault of peer
pressure to drink alcohol. A short time later, she tried mari-
juana. Like so many, this was only the beginning, and Sarah's
path led to unimaginable sorrows. Initially, she would stop
using drugs and alcohol for short periods of time, but then
she would again succumb to temptation. She went through
countless stints of being in and out of rehab centers. Guilt,

shame, and self condemnation took over her life, and hopelessness prevailed. At her lowest point, she lived on the streets as a heroin addict, prostituting to support her habit. Sarah did eventually come into victory, but it was not without a long battle. In addition to the physical battle of addiction, it was a process to overcome the guilt and shame, which are always so prevalent in the midst of our failures. Praise God that His love and power is well able to reach us no matter where we are!

While your self-disappointment may not be as drastic as Sarah's, the inward struggles can be the same. We fight disappointment with our unmet expectations of ourselves: lost investments and relationships, being older and not where we desired to be in our life, decisions we have made that in hindsight proved wrong, etc. Disappointment with self is perhaps the most paralyzing of all disappointments. It becomes more difficult to make decisions, open our hearts to relationships, or look at the future with expectation. We get caught in its swirl and it taints our lives with hopelessness. Self-disappointment steals hope like no other issue because it subtly transitions our focus away from God and onto self, which is all consuming. When we become trapped in this place of deception, we live trying to protect ourselves from the pain it causes, and when this is unsuccessful, it leads to further despair.

To defeat disappointment, we must bring our focus back to Jesus and His amazing love for us! As our eyes behold who

He is, instead of what we are not, we will again be filled with hope. He covers all of our failures, and at times, the things we have defined as failure are defined differently as Christ broadens our vision and we see things with His eyes.

Be careful in this place of disappointment, because the sin of unbelief can creep in very quickly and open the door to self-pity, robbing us of joy, confidence, motivation, and passion. Self-focus results in unbelief and fills us with shame, condemnation, guilt, and even self-hatred. But when we receive and walk in the true revelation of God's love, it will always leave us focused on Him and filled with gratitude. When we sin, we feel the sting of guilt, and we are disappointed by our actions, but when we receive God's loving correction and forgiveness, hope arises and we return our focus back to Him.

THE NATURE OF SELF

The conscience is the dimension of our soul that brings awareness. It was created in order for man to experience

---

To defeat disappointment, we must bring our focus back to Jesus and His amazing love for us! As our eyes behold who He is, instead of what we are not, we will again be filled with hope.

God. Self-consciousness is the awareness of evil within us, which began in the Garden of Eden (Genesis 3:7), and it lies within the region of our corrupted or defiled soul. Our conscience is where the enemy assaults us with his accusations. Prior to partaking of the tree of the knowledge of good and evil, Adam and Eve were "naked and not ashamed" (Genesis 2:25). They were alive unto God in perfect and unbroken fellowship with Him in spirit, soul, and body. Sin did not exist in their nature, which allowed them to be free from self-focus or self-consciousness. They were completely free from even an *awareness* of sin and guilt.

However, as soon as they disobeyed God, their eyes were opened and they knew that they were naked. In other words, they became aware of the difference between good and evil. They had been aware of their freedom to choose, but now they were aware of the ability to choose evil, and the immediate result was this dimension of self-consciousness, which brought guilt, shame, and death.

God's promise of death within (Genesis 2:17) came to pass. Their spirit man experienced an **immediate** death, or separation from perfect fellowship with God. Their soul entered into a **progressive** state of dying or being corrupted with evil (Genesis 6:5), and their body received the sentence of **ultimate** death (Genesis 3:19).

Now, with the entrance of sin into the human race and the resulting self-awareness, the enemy had access to influence mankind. Every form of evil and darkness that was within the devil began to insert itself into humanity. Sin and self-consciousness became the battle-ground within man to keep him from fellowship with God.

THE SECOND ADAM

The New Testament calls Jesus the second – or last – Adam (1 Corinthians 15:45, 47). Because sin came through man, sin also had to be paid for by man (see Romans 5:12-19). Jesus came into the world without the two characteristics the first Adam (and consequently all of mankind) possessed after the fall. First, Jesus did not have the fallen nature of sin because He was conceived of the Holy Spirit (see Luke 1:31, 35). Secondly, because He did not have sin, He did not have self-consciousness.

Because of His sinless life, He was the perfect sacrifice for sin. When Jesus gave His life on the cross, He not only paid for sin, He *became* sin. And because of His sacrifice, we who have placed our trust, hope, and faith in Him **have now literally become the righteousness of God in Christ** (2 Corinthians 5:21)!

What does this mean? It means that the death sentence in the Garden of Eden has been reversed. "For the law of the Spirit of life in Christ Jesus has made me free from the law of sin and death" (Romans 8:2). As believers, when we receive Jesus by faith, we **immediately** are made alive unto God in our spirit man (see Ephesians 2:1, 5, 6). We are **progressively** being transformed into His image and **ultimately** we will receive a new and glorified body (see Romans 8:29 and Philippians 3:21).

We are now restored to perfect fellowship with God. Sin had been paid for, and we are free and in perfect standing with God! John said, "Whoever has been born of God does not sin, for His (Jesus) seed remains in him; and he cannot sin, because he has been born of God" (1 John 3:9).

John is talking about our resurrected, perfected spirit man. It is imperative that we are grounded in this truth because the degree in which we believe that we are in perfect relationship to God in our spirit man is the degree to which we can receive the work of sanctification within our soul. It is also the degree to which we will be able to resist the accusations of the accuser.

SANCTIFICATION

One day we will receive a new body but while we remain in these earthly bodies, we live the life of sanctification. Sanctification is the process in which we, as perfectly righteous sons and daughters of God, are transformed into the image of God within our souls. Hebrews 10:14 says, "By one offering He has perfected forever those who are being sanctified" (NKJV).

The degree in which we believe that we are in perfect relationship to God in our spirit man is the degree to which we can receive the work of sanctification within our soul. It is also the degree to which we will be able to resist the accusations of the accuser.

Do you know what it is like to tell God "I am sorry for having to say I am sorry for doing the same thing over and over again?" We all do. But Proverbs 24:16 says that even though the righteous fall seven times, they rise again. Why is that? It is because God is the One working in us to perfect what He started (see Hebrews 12:2).

New birth and sanctification is the work of God. If on any level you don't believe this, you will strive to be pleasing and acceptable to God based on your own efforts rather than on the finished work of the cross (see Galatians 3:1-5). As a born again child of God, you will never be more accepted than you already are!

GUILT VS. SHAME

The reason people feel guilt when they sin or make a mistake is because they are guilty! As previously stated, our conscience was originally created to only give awareness of

God. Due to sin, the enemy now has access to bring accusation against us, and our fallen conscience is the focal point of warfare between the devil and God. **Your response to any sin or mistake is what will determine your level of victory over being disappointed with yourself.**

When we sin, guilt hits our conscience, and immediately two forces come to us. The enemy is there to accuse, bring condemnation and shame, and ultimately drive us from the presence of God, which brings hopelessness. Holy Spirit is there, too. He convicts us of our guilt but at the same time, He is there to clothe, heal, and love us. He draws us to Himself, which removes guilt and replaces disappointment with hope (1 John 1:9).

The marvelous love and grace of God is infinitely greater than the gross darkness of sin (see Romans 5:20). Often, it is during these battles of the soul and conscience that you least feel like drawing near to God. But these are some of the most vital times to run to Him (see Hebrews 10:19-23)! Sometimes we don't run to Him because we feel we have disappointed God, but you can never disappoint Him. He knows every aspect of your heart and soul, and He is not surprised when we make a mistake. He does not have any expectation of us that we can disappoint; He knows you better than you do! So, again, run to Him! Repent, release the guilt, and refuse to pick up the shame. Find the truth of yourself in Him and be made whole as you gaze into His eyes of love.

Sonship vs. Servanthood

The revelation of true sonship, as opposed to simply being a servant, will establish your position with God like nothing else. A son with the full revelation of his Father's love never feels inferior, but a servant always feels second-rate. Galatians 4:1-7 paints the accurate picture of a son's heart.

> Now I say, as long as the heir is a child, he does not differ at all from a slave although he is owner of everything, but he is under guardians and managers until the date set by the father. So also we, while we were children, were held in bondage under the elemental things of the world. But when the fullness of the time came, God sent forth His Son, born of a woman, born under the Law, so that He might redeem those who were under the Law, that we might receive the adoption as sons. Because you are sons, God has sent forth the Spirit of His Son into our hearts, crying, "Abba! Father!" Therefore you are no longer a slave, but a son; and if a son, then an heir through God (NASB).

Verse six reveals the God-given, deep cry within for relationship with our loving Father. Without that revelation, we

A son with the full revelation of his Father's love never feels inferior, but a servant always feels second-rate.

will believe that our good standing with God is based upon our performance rather than His adoption of us. The older brother in the parable of the prodigal son (Luke 15:11-32) is a great example of this mindset. He continued to live in the father's house but he never realized all the blessings he had as a son. The repentant prodigal, however, experienced the depth of his father's love as soon as he returned home.

I was blessed with a wonderful earthly father and because his love toward me was so great, I was never envious when I saw him display love to my siblings. It was not even an issue. For every child of God, it should be the same. The enemy always tempts us to compare ourselves with others. When we see giftings and success in others, we often feel inferior. But when our value is firmly placed in our heavenly Father's love for us, we are satisfied and secure.

Of course, the greatest example we have of being established in a Father's love is Jesus (see John 5:20). He was the perfect Son. As *perfected* sons of God, we can and should experience the same security that Jesus did. One of the most powerful Scriptures is when Jesus prayed that we would know the Father loves us as much as He loves Jesus (see John 17:23).

Often, there are those who love the Lord so much, but don't have the revelation of sonship. Living under the law, they continue to "try and get it right" to please God, but also feel they always fall a little short. God is pleased with you!

Jesus is the lens of love you are viewed through, and God loves and takes pleasure in you just because you are HIS!

I delight in my grandson, and when he comes to visit, he always likes to make my morning coffee. I'll sit in the recliner and he will carefully bring in his gift of coffee and present it to me with hopeful expectation of my approval... he is never disappointed. The coffee he brings me is ALWAYS perfect. It doesn't matter if it is thick as mud, swimming in grounds, has too much or too little sugar... it is perfect because it is presented to me by the one in whom I take pleasure.

As you present yourself to God, you are perfect! Regardless of the condition in which you are presented, you are the one in whom God delights, you are His and you please Him to no end! You can relax when you look into the eyes of your heavenly Father because you will never see disappointment, only love, acceptance, and joy that you're with Him.

The love that God the Father has for you is the greatest revelation available to defeat disappointment with self. Believe it now. Receive it now. It is truth!

THE POWER OF TRUE HUMILITY

One of the greatest keys to victory over self-disappointment is to live and walk in the revelation of humility. True humility is born from the revelation of Father's love. You see, humility is not thinking less of ourselves, but rather thinking of ourselves less! To be truly humble is to be in agreement with what God says about us, which always causes a heart of gratitude and focus on God.

False humility focuses on self and the shortcomings within. Numbers 12:3 says, "The man Moses was very humble, more than any man on the face of the earth" (NASB). Who wrote that? Moses did! This was not a statement of arrogance; it was agreement with God. Anytime we believe less than what God says about us, it is an offense to the cross. The price paid for all of humanity determines our value.

CONCLUSION

At times, most everyone has had the feeling that God loves others more. Most have experienced the feeling that God does not love them at all or, at best, He is very mad at them. These are lies from the enemy, which contain unbelief at their very core. Settle this in your heart now, once and for all – you are loved. You are accepted and righteous before your God.

"What shall we say about such wonderful things as these? If God is for us, who can ever be against us" (Romans 8:31 NLT)? If God is not against you, then don't be against yourself!

The lyrics to "How He Loves Us" summarize it well:

> I don't have time to maintain these
> regrets when I think about the way
> He loves us
> Oh how he loves us
> Oh how he loves us
> Oh how he loves!

— Kim Walker-Smith

HEART CHECK-UP

1. Have there been times that you've been disappointed with yourself?

2. Have you allowed the Holy Spirit into those areas and received HIS definition of you? What was the result?

3. Has your focus been on you (which leads to defeat and hopelessness), or are your eyes on Him, the One who delights in you and calls you perfect?

PRAYER

Father, I submit myself to You for a shift in my perspective. Forgive me for focusing on myself and losing sight of You in the midst of disappointment. Today, I choose to believe You! I renounce the lies that have condemned me, and I embrace Your absolute, everlasting, unchanging love for me. God, honestly, this is beyond my comprehension, and I want Your love to be more than what I hear... I desire to experience Your love and have it saturate every bit of my being! Thank You, Father... I love You, too!

(Take some time here and allow yourself to soak in His love for you. Choose to lay down your defenses or doubts, and just accept His love. Give all of yourself to Him; He loves all of you.)

4

DISAPPOINTMENT
with OTHERS

LIFE WITHOUT RELATIONSHIP with others is not life as God intended. The very nature of God (Love Himself) is expressed through relationships. When sin entered the world, not only was our relationship with God broken, but also our relationship with each other. It did not take long for hatred to manifest, and as a result Cain killed his brother Abel (see Genesis 4:8).

Through the redemptive work of the cross, God not only restored man to relationship with Him, but He began the restoration of our relationships with each other. While in the spirit man we are all fully restored to relationship with God, there is that part of our soul, which is in a growing process. It is the same with our relationships with one another. In Christ, we are to know one another after the spirit (see 2 Corinthians 5:16). But since our soul is a work in progress, so is our ability to rightly relate to one another.

When Jesus finished His work on the earth, He summed up the commandments for us before He left.

> A new command I give to you, that you love one another; **as I have loved you**, that you also love one another. By this all will know that you are My disciples, if you have love for one another.
>
> — John 13:34-35

Since loving relationships are the key to the world coming to know Jesus, it is no wonder that the enemy fights to destroy relationships more than anything else. When we add to this the fact that we are all imperfect, we see the unavoidable reality of being disappointed by people.

As we look at various relationships with different groups of people, the root cause of disappointment will be the same in each case: unmet expectations. Whether they are realistic or not, the result is the same: disappointment.

Broken relationships are one of life's most painful disappointments. They cause injury, grief, and pain, and often leave us to suffer from misconceptions. Past experiences in disappointing relationships often leave us cynical and over-ly critical in our judgment of others. We begin to see each other as a collection of our perceptions and misconceived ideas, never able to look beyond our clouded viewpoint to see someone as they truly are. According to our perception, people are delightful and good, or evil, malicious, and cow-ardly. This "all or nothing" mentality is the very nature of adolescent thinking.

Certainly, it's right to have certain expectations of oth-ers. A wife should expect her husband to love her. A parent should expect their child to love and obey them – that is God's design. But as imperfect people, we can't place de-mands of perfection on others.

When our hearts are healed by the love of God, He brings us to the place where we see others as they really are, without becoming critical or cynical. That is why Paul prayed that our love would abound more and more in order for us to perceive correctly (Philippians 1:9-10). Pure and perfect dis-cernment only comes when we are motivated and controlled by pure love.

This leads us to the next problematic area, which is de-fining what love is. We all have our own ideas of what love looks like, and since we are all growing in the knowledge of God's love, our ideas can be vastly different. **We each cre-ate expectations based on our perspective of love.** When those expectations are not met, or worse, not agreed upon, we are doomed for disappointment. When we agree upon what love looks like, we are more open to forgive a love failure. But when we do not, the challenge is greater.

LOVE FROM JESUS' PERSPECTIVE

> But Jesus did not commit Himself to them, because He knew all men, and had no need that anyone should testify of man, for He knew what was in man.
>
> — John 2:24-25

In this passage, "them" refers to those who believed in Jesus. What does it mean that Jesus did not commit Himself to these people? Certainly Jesus was committed to mankind – He loved us so much that He gave His life for us.

In this verse, the Greek word for commit is *pisteuō*, which is translated as "to believe" 239 times in the New Testament. It is from the same root word as *faith*. Jesus did not have faith in man because He knew what was in them! He never based His love for man on anything they did. In other words, He never placed demands or unrealistic expectations upon people. By not placing demands upon them, He was free to completely love them as they were!

Jesus' love was so perfect that He could see everyone as they truly were and yet never despair of anyone. His love was based on His revelation of God's love for Him as well as

> Jesus' love was so perfect that He could see everyone as they truly were and yet never despair of anyone. His love was based on His revelation of God's love for Him as well as others.

others. Jesus told His disciples that He had loved them as the Father had loved Him (see John 15:9)!

That is why Jesus said we are to love others as **He loved us.** We often try to love people as Jesus loves them, but we can't give away what we don't have. We must continue to ask for deeper revelation of His love to us, so that it can flow out of us to others.

When we truly begin to love others **the way Jesus loves us,** we will eliminate the vast majority of our disappointments because we will stop placing demands and unrealistic expectations on people. That does not mean we will not be hurt. I believe that Jesus' heart was hurt many times. However, His heart did not become sick or hopeless, because He had no illusions or unreal expectations. His love was perfect! **There is a vast difference between having pain in your heart and having a sick heart.**

As you look at specific relationships, keep these truths in mind. Ask God to show you where you love others based on *your* perspective of love as opposed to His. Allow Him to heal every area of your heart that may be sick. **The key to**

healing is never about seeing others change. The key is always to allow God to change us. In doing so, not only will you be healed, but you will also see healing come to broken relationships in your life.

I pray that God will touch your heart in the place that is in desperate need of His healing. Let Him lay the ax to the root of your disappointment and also allow the Holy Spirit to heal and cleanse you of the fruit we discussed in chapter one.

Family

I am convinced that there is no place where our love is tested and Christ-likeness is formed in us more than within the family. It is within the confines of our homes that most of our "junk" surfaces. It is also where we have the greatest opportunity to grow in love and be conformed into His image (see Romans 8:29).

Your Spouse

Marriages are falling apart in epidemic proportions. We are in desperate need of fresh revelation and commitment in marriage. I once heard it said that husbands marry thinking that their wives will never change, and wives marry thinking they can change their husbands. While this is not always true, unfortunately this mindset does exist. It reveals an expectation based on human love rather than the love of God, and both are a set up for disappointment and heartache.

My wife and I have been married for thirty-two years. For the most part, it has been amazing, but to say that we have never been disappointed in each other would simply be a lie. I have learned that the times I held onto disappointment only revealed that my love was based upon her satisfying my demands. The end result was a sick heart for me.

Unfortunately, there have been times that I refused to let God work in me, and through those choices, I allowed the enemy to harden my heart. Jesus said the root issue of divorce is a hard heart (see Matthew 19:8). Until I repented of my pride, my heart remained sick. Once I let the love of God convict me and bring me into agreement with Him, I was healed and free to love with His love. Freedom came to love with His love rather than my own.

If you are struggling in your marriage now, be still before the Lord. Do not cover up the pain. Open your heart wide and ask Him to fill you with His love. Ask Him to speak the truth to your heart about its condition. Be willing to break before Him. Silence the voice of the accuser, and allow Holy Spirit to heal you.

If you are living in the pain of a broken marriage or divorce, know that God can and will heal your heart. Get with God and friends, and allow the healing to happen. The enemy will lie and tell you that the pain will never end. It will.

If you are living in the pain of a broken marriage or divorce, know that God can and will heal your heart. Get with God and friends, and allow the healing to happen. The enemy will lie and tell you that the pain will never end. It will.

Right now, know that I believe for you, and I am praying for you to have hope restored. God's mercies are new every morning and His faithfulness reaches to the heavens. He is good! He will heal your soul!

OUR CHILDREN

God has taught me more about His love through my kids than anything else. In her teen years, our oldest daughter went into rebellion. Every time my wife and I thought it could not get worse, it did. One day, as I poured out my heart to God, I realized I was quite angry with my daughter on many levels. I was angry that she had messed up our perfect little family, and I was angry that she devastated our personal relationship. *I missed her.* My heart was broken with disappointment.

In the midst of my anger, God spoke to me, "So, are you going to crucify her or get on the cross for her?" I was undone, and I began to weep uncontrollably. I knew that God had exposed my conditional love.

It was still quite some time before the circumstances surrounding our daughter changed. *But I changed.* Disappointment was replaced with hope. Instead of fighting against her, I began to fight *for* her, and not for myself. Instead of being angry, I became broken hearted for her. God's love changed me and healed my sick heart, and in the end, our faithful God reached her heart too. He is good!

If you have broken relationships with your children, immediately begin to let God heal your heart and fill you with His love. Maybe you are estranged because of your faults. Let Him heal you from shame and guilt. It is not too late – He can and will restore! Believe God, and receive hope!

THE FATHER WOUND

In our culture, the epidemic of broken homes and absent fathers has dealt more devastation to innocent hearts than anything else. In over twenty years of counseling, it is by far the most common root of pain I have dealt with. In the midst of hearts broken over poor or absent fathers, the enemy has caused those affected to have a distorted and unhealthy view of God the Father. If this is you, let this be a time of healing!

In John 14:9, Jesus said that whoever has seen Him, has seen the Father. Many are able to relate to Jesus as the Son of God, but they cannot make the connection that He IS God – they cannot see God the Father as having the same characteristics as Jesus. This verse holds a great key to heal your heart from Father wounds. Begin to embrace the truth that everything you see in Jesus is the same nature and character of God the Father.

> He is the sole expression of the glory of God [the Light-being, the out-raying or radiance of the divine], and **He is the perfect imprint and very image of [God's] nature.**
>
> — Hebrews 1:3 AMP (emphasis added)

Let God the Father reveal Himself to you now. You may need to go through a process of forgiving your earthly father, but it will set you free to receive the love of your *heavenly* Father!

Father, I pray for the one reading this whose heart has been broken by their earthly father. Reveal Yourself to them now. I break the power of the enemy's lies, concerning who You are. Heal their heart in Jesus' name!

THE CHURCH

We don't have to look very far into the chronicles of church history to see how much devastation the body of Christ has inflicted upon itself. The atrocities the church has inflicted upon itself are almost unimaginable, and unfortunately, it continues today. Church splits are as common as new church plants – too often they are one in the same thing.

It is likely that you have been wounded by the church, or perhaps even devastated. We have an expectation that church should be a safe place and it is very disappointing when we find that is not always the case. Shepherds commissioned to care for the sheep instead inflict injury at times and then we certainly see wounded sheep that cause harm to the rest of the flock! Few have been left unscathed, but we cannot stay in the place of disappointment and hurt. When others do not represent the heart of God well, we must forgive them and look to God, who *always* represents Himself well!

Since the ascension of Jesus after His resurrection, there has been no greater spiritual war than the battle for unity within the body of Christ. Satan knows that his greatest defeats happen not when we have all night prayer meetings (as important and powerful as they are), but when we simply love one another. The world is starving for love, and we are the only ones to represent Him in the earth.

LET THE HEALING BEGIN – MY STORY

My wife and I had the privilege of shepherding a local fellowship in a small town in the Midwest for nine years. Those years hold some of my fondest memories. Testimonies abound of all the lives saved, lives changed, and miracles that God did. We had many joyous times in the Lord and with the family of God there. They were and still are amazing people.

There were difficult times as well. Broken relationships are the most painful thing that any of us deal with, and we had our share. This is not to point fingers; each individual has a perspective in each case, and there is a measure of validity in each one. No one is perfect. Our aim should never be to prove who is wrong and who is right, and that is not my aim now. Our highest aim is to walk in the love of the God. One time the Lord said to me, "You are right, but you are not righteous." That is another way of saying you are in pride.

After nine years, we made the decision to leave the church as its pastor. At first, there was some relief – it felt good to get out from under the pressure and constant warfare. But relief is never the same as healing. In fact, over the next eighteen months the pain that had built up in my heart surfaced. I had not realized it, but one disappointment after another had its accumulative effect, and the fruit of my sick heart began to manifest. Cynicism became a constant companion, and hopelessness stole my passion for God.

On the outside, I was functioning fine. I even continued to preach and minister under the anointing (the gifts and callings of God are without repentance). But on the inside, I hurt, and it felt like I was dying. One night, at my lowest point, I curled up in bed and with tears streaming down my face, I prayed, "God, all I can say is please don't give up on me." Praise God, He did not!

From that point, I got serious with God; I allowed Him to deal with the sickness in my heart and to convict me of everything and anything He wanted to. The end result was that He poured His love into me. He restored my passion for Him. He restored my hope and healed my heart.

Let me encourage you to, first, get with God and **let the healing begin**... Now. Precious saint, there is no disappointment that God cannot heal. Stop listening to the accuser and, by all means, stop agreeing with him! Blame – even if you are right – will never bring healing; it only magnifies the sick heart.

Next, don't let the enemy keep you from the body of Christ. Isolation is dangerous – we need each other. Where possible, seek reconciliation with others (see Romans 12:18). When it seems a relationship cannot be mended, walk in love and never give up. God will make a way if your heart is willing. Let Him place hope back in your heart!

Don't let the enemy keep you from the body of Christ. Isolation is dangerous – we need each other. Where possible, seek reconciliation with others. When it seems a relationship cannot be mended, walk in love and never give up. God will make a way if your heart is willing.

Now I present you with a challenge from a lesson I learned while watching one of my favorite movies, *The Last Samurai*. The word samurai means servant. He was the leader of a group of warriors and villages in ancient Japan. The samurai existed to serve the emperor and the people; he was willing to die for them, and he was always at the front of every battle, leading the way. This should be a picture of every pastor and ministry leader.

During one scene in the movie, the village people were having a festive celebration at night, and Ninja warriors attacked them by surprise. The first words heard in the movie were, "Protect the samurai!" What a picture of the body of Christ protecting its leaders.

There are so many wonderful leaders and members in the body of Christ. However, there is too often the attacking of one another. Let's raise the bar, and let's fight *together* instead of against each other. Let's allow God to take our love to a higher level than we have ever known. Let's all have the heart of the samurai and protect the samurai!

Conclusion

I have only mentioned a few areas of relationship. There are many others, but the principles are the same. Never underestimate the power and importance of any relationship. Every interaction with another human being is an opportunity for the love of God to be expressed. It's your purpose – you exist to be a representative of His love and glory in the earth (see Habakuk 2:14, John 20:21).

Don't allow the enemy to steal from you anymore. Allow the Lord to heal your heart from disappointment. You can do it! He died to heal us, and you are worth it – He made that decision.

HEART CHECK-UP

1. Are you carrying the stones of resentment and bit terness in your heart because someone disappointed you? Whar are you planning on doing about it?

2. Have you felt betrayed or had a need that was not met by those close to you?

3. Do you struggle with people not living up to your expectations?

4. Are you ready to release the hardness this creates in your heart, and allow God to bring you healing and freedom?

PRAYER

Lord, search me and show me any areas of unforgiveness, resentment, and bitterness in my heart. I choose to be free, so I choose to forgive _____. I renounce my judgments toward them and I forgive the places they have not met my expectations. Father, forgive me for holding on to offense; I release my resentment and bitterness and I ask for Your love to take their place. Make my heart soft again, and remind me to look to You when others disappoint me and to quickly forgive and love them, as You have loved me. Lord, please continue to give me deeper revelation of Your grace and love, so that I will be a releaser of Your grace and love to others.

5

ETERNAL PERSPECTIVE

WE HAVE ALREADY ESTABLISHED that things seldom, if ever, turn out exactly like we think they will. The same Jesus who promised us life in abundance also said that we would have tribulation in this world (John 16:33). No one escapes trials and hardships or escapes the reality of disappointments. So how do we walk in the abundant life that Jesus promised without being overcome with hopelessness because of disappointment?

THE POWER OF PERSPECTIVE

Your perspective is your reality, whether or not it is truth. We all have different perspectives, and to the one perceiving, theirs is true. That is why it is imperative that we live with an *eternal* perspective, which means that we see from God's viewpoint.

ETERNAL OUTLOOK

> Therefore we do not lose heart. Even though our outward man is perishing, yet the inward man is being renewed day by day. For our light affliction, which is but for a moment, is working for us a far more exceeding and eternal weight of glory, while we do not look at the things which are seen, but at the things which are not seen. For the things which are seen are temporary, but the things which are not seen are eternal.
>
> — 2 Corinthians 4:16-18 NASB
> (emphasis added)

In this passage, the apostle Paul makes some amazing statements. Here is a man who had suffered tremendously, even stating that it was so much that he was "burdened beyond measure, above strength, so that we despaired even of life" (see 2 Corinthians 1:8). Yet now, he claimed that it was only "light affliction." How can this be?

It was because he never lost sight of the reality of eternity. His inward man was never overcome by disappointment and hopelessness. Not only did he look forward to his ultimate eternal home, but he also knew how to live in eternal glory now. He was filled with hope while in the midst of trials. His hope was not dependant on the circumstances of this life, but rather on the unseen eternal realities.

One of the clearest distinctions between a temporal and eternal perspective is in 1 Thessalonians 4:13, "But we do not want you to be uninformed, brethren, about those who are asleep, so that you will not grieve as do the rest who have no hope." This verse presents the contrasting views of those with hope and those without hope in the midst of the sorrow of death. In the midst of death, there is sorrow for believer and non-believer alike. The difference lies in the fact the believers have hope! Why? Because we know that this life is temporal. Paul said it this way, "If all we get out of Christ is a little inspiration for a few short years, we're a pretty sorry lot" (1 Corinthians 15:19 The Message).

Abraham is a great example of an Old Testament man who maintained an eternal perspective. He was mightily blessed of the Lord in the earth – he was wealthy, his children prospered, and he received amazing promises and the fulfillment of those promises while living in the earth. And yet, "He looked for a city which hath foundations whose builder and maker is God" (Hebrews 11:10 KJV). With all of the blessings he enjoyed in this life, he never lost sight of the realities of eternity.

This kind of eternal perspective, which is founded in a steadfast belief and trust in the sovereignty and goodness of God, assures our hearts that even if we don't have a full understanding, our faith is not shaken. It is from this vantage point that we can live as more than just survivors. We can live as overcomers.

MORE THAN CONQUERORS

While we maintain an eternal perspective, it is equally important that we not embrace an escapist mindset, which says that the best we can hope for is to simply hang on until either we die or the rapture. This is a defeatist perspective that actually opposes a life of victorious faith and overcoming. It interprets "enduring" as merely holding on instead of *persevering*.

Enduring has no hope *in this life* while persevering embraces the promises of God through faith. The psalmist said it this way, "I would have lost heart unless I had believed that I would see the goodness of the Lord in the land of the living" (Psalm 27:13).

When we embrace an escapist mindset, the enemy has gained a foothold in our usefulness to the kingdom of God in the earth. The enemy knows that he is defeated, but it is through deceptions like these that he minimize our effectiveness to implement the victory of the finished work of the cross. This mindset of escapism will cause us to back away from the fight of faith and fail to embrace the promises of God. It quickly becomes a stronghold of unbelief.

This does not mean that we love the things of this world as 1 John 2:15 exhorts us not to do. The word "world" comes

Enduring has no hope *in this life* while persevering embraces the promises of God through faith. The psalmist said it this way, "I would have lost heart unless I had believed that I would see the goodness of the Lord in the land of the living" (Psalm 27:13).

from the Greek word *kosmos,* which refers to the temporal world's systems and values. Jesus said, "His kingdom is not of this world" (John 18:36). We can embrace and enjoy everything God promised to us in this life, while still having a kingdom mindset (1 Timothy 6:17). When we have a proper eternal mindset, we will not be ensnared by the enemy's deceptions and overcome with hopelessness.

THE REALITY OF LOSS

I would be remiss if I did not acknowledge the reality of loss in this life. We live in a fallen world. Tragedy and injustice abound. But we must apply an eternal perspective to all that we see. Psalm 73 is a wonderful example of a man who temporarily lost his eternal perspective and became sick at heart.

But as for me, my feet had almost stumbled;
My steps had nearly slipped.

For I was envious of the boastful,
When I saw the prosperity of the wicked....

When I thought how to understand this,
It was too painful for me—
Until I went into the sanctuary of God;
Then I understood their end.

Surely You set them in slippery places;
You cast them down to destruction.
Oh, how they are brought to desolation, as in a
moment!
They are utterly consumed with terrors.
As a dream when one awakes,
So, Lord, when You awake,
You shall despise their image.

Thus my heart was grieved,
And I was vexed in my mind.
I was so foolish and ignorant;
I was like a beast before You.
Nevertheless I am continually with You;
You hold me by my right hand.
You will guide me with Your counsel,
And afterward receive me to glory.

Whom have I in heaven but You?
And there is none upon earth that I desire besides
You.
My flesh and my heart fail;
But God is the strength of my heart and my por-
tion forever.

For indeed, those who are far from You shall per-
ish;
You have destroyed all those who desert You for
harlotry.
But it is good for me to draw near to God;
I have put my trust in the Lord GOD,
That I may declare all Your works.

— Psalm 73:2-3, 16-28

In this Psalm, the writer had lost sight of the goodness of God as he watched the wicked prosper and the righteous suffer. But he went into the presence of God and received God's eternal perspective, and from that place, his heart was not only healed, but also broken for the wicked. He not only gained God's perspective, more importantly, he gained God's heart!

You may be reading this now in the midst of horrible loss. If your heart is filled with despair and hopelessness, I encourage you to draw near to God, spend time in His presence, and let Him heal your heart. Healing your heart does not mean immediate removal of pain – grieving is a process – but it does mean you can have hope restored. His perspective, His heart and, most of all, His love will give you hope.

Hope does not disappoint, because the love of God has been poured out in our hearts by the Holy Spirit who was given to us (see Romans 5:5). You will arise victoriously. You will hope again. You will dream again.

LIVE IN PEACE

God has called us to live in peace and to pursue peace.

And let the peace (soul harmony which comes) from Christ rule (act as umpire continually) in your hearts [deciding and **settling with finality all questions that arise in your minds**, in that peaceful state] to which as [members of Christ's] one body you were also called [to live]. And be thankful (appreciative), [giving praise to God always].

— Colossians 3:15 AMP
(emphasis added)

Out of that place of peace, we have the opportunity to be still before God, and allow His healing work to manifest in our hearts.

We live in the greatest days of opportunity for kingdom advancement since the world began. The accompanying warfare is greater than ever, but while the world grows darker, the light shines brighter than ever! It is truly time for God's people to arise and shine (Isaiah 60:1-2). The darkness is passing away, and the true light is already shining (1 John 2:8).

The devil knows his time is short. Don't let him steal your hope, faith, and passion any longer. Your best days are ahead of you. Let them begin *now*. Hope is a good thing – maybe the best of things. You have a choice, you can get busy living, or get busy dying. Come on.... What do you say? Let's get busy living!

HEART CHECK-UP

1. From what perspective are you living?

2. Are you easily shaken by circumstances?

3. Do you find that you are often troubled, fearful, or anxious? If so, begin today to live from a higher vantage point, the eternal perspective.

PRAYER

Lord, forgive me; too often I find that my eyes stay in the place of "in this world you will have trouble" instead of lifting my eyes to see YOU, who have overcome the world. I will lift up my eyes to behold You in the midst of my circumstances. I will stand in the unchanging truth of who You are and the Words You have spoken. I will form my life around Your truth so that my core becomes unshakable, securely anchored in Your goodness and faithfulness. Lord, I want to see with Your eyes and join with You to release heaven in this earth. I am seated with You in heavenly places, and I shall not be moved!

Additional copies of this book and other book titles
from XP Publishing
are available at the "store" at xpministries.com

BULK ORDERS:

We have bulk/wholesale prices for stores and ministries.
Please contact: resource@xpministries.com.

www.XPpublishing.com
A Department of XP Ministries